M000312396

life between naps

Jim Noonan

MorningNoonanNight Publishing

life between naps
Copyright © 2016 Jim Noonan
Published by MorningNoonanNight Publishing
All rights reserved.

Cover created by Thomas Kearns whose expertise in graphic design saved the day.

ISBN: 978-0-692-59895-5

For Cathy, who is still nice.

Contents

Acknowledgments

First and foremost, I wanna thank MorningNoonanNight Publishing for taking a chance on the little book with big aspirations. I also wanna thank my wife who said, "Let's do it!" Then said, "Why's it taking so long?" Followed by, "Are you finished?!" And finally, "Thank god it's over." Without her pep talk, we never would've had kids. She was also a crucial part of motivating me to get this book done. To all the family and friends who kept asking me when this "book'll" be finished, here it is! I thank and love you all.

From Beneath

Growing up in Michigan, I had two fears: large white vans with tinted windows, and whales.

I'm not a big fan of the ocean; quite frankly I think it's overrated. I mean have you ever had to sit and listen to someone who just got back from a trip to Hawaii or Pensacola? Every other word is some sorta grossly orgasmic epiphany about their place on this earth, like, "The ocean at sunset made me realize that we're all just small cogs in the machine of life" or "The fragility of life is controlled by the tiny heartbeat of a panda's whisper." If you're lucky, these delusional sandcombers might bless you with an outrageous analogy like, "Watching the waves crash into the sand (pause for dramatic breath) made me realize (pause for another goddamn dramatic breath) just how similar the career arcs of Nicolas Cage and Jesus are." People lose their minds for the ocean. I, on the other hand, am not one of those people. I find nothing calm or awe-inspiring about a cold, dark, and vastly unexplored playroom for known and unknown creatures such as Sharktopus and whales. The kind who harbor a taste for human flesh and the ability to swallow you whole. But I didn't always think like this.

Before 1992, I was scared of normal things like liver, sparklers, and cats. I thought awful ways to die would be a car accident or melting in a house fire. And then I saw this video where a woman was swimming with a whale, and suddenly it takes hold of her foot and drags her down fifty feet, while her husband records the whole thing on video! Ultimately she lived, claiming that the whale was "just playing," but my idea of horrific deaths shifted after that—big time! Now I had to deal with fears of death from beneath!

The thought of being swallowed, tugged, and chewed by a two hundred ton beast was so paralyzing, I couldn't imagine *ever* stepping a foot in the ocean. It's a nightmare scenario, which includes shock, drowning, dismemberment, gnawing-slashing razor-sharp teeth, helplessness, and regret. This catapulted into the top spot of terror, the coup de grace of death, and it lived somewhere out there, deep in the ocean.

I was twenty years old and thirty thousand feet above sea level the first time I laid eyes on the watery abyss. Looking out that small double-paned window, I watched as the water taunted me with malevolent shapes of terror. Every shadow, wave, and flicker was a potential monster. I watched nervously as they followed and waited for my plane to drop out of the sky.

Two weeks later I was clinging to the inside of a four-man dinghy as my friends maneuvered slowly through the calm fjords of the Nordic coastline. Our destination, which was reachable only by boat or yak, was a little peninsula where family and friends were treating a couple of Americans to a Norwegian picnic. We spent hours basking in the sun, eating, and exploring the eclectic terrain. I watched as the seasoned Norwegian men fished for nothing and drank for everything. I listened to the women cackle in their native tongue and smiled as the children licked melted chocolate bars from the tips of their fingers. Nothing was ever gonna beat that moment, that experience, that...

Wait! What the...? Oh no, are they getting out skis?

I avoided eye contact with anyone who showed association to the boats huddled along the coastline. I took several trips into the woods and even faked a case of diarrhea in order to escape an invitation to ski. After what seemed like hours of neglecting friends and acting awkward, I heard the rumor that we might be packing up and leaving. Exhilarated by the possibility of getting back to a drier chunk of land, I headed into the woods one last time to relieve myself and lay scent on the lush fauna. I was midstream when a rustle of the bushes behind me gave way to a firm calloused hand atop my shoulder. "You are up?" said a man with Aquavit breath. "We leave after you ski."

I looked out over the water; it was still and not overwhelming. Surrounded by mountains on all sides, the water seemed more like a lake than ocean. I looked the man in the face, bit my bottom lip, and nodded. He smiled, patted me on the back, and pointed to a wet suit. "Put da suit on. Da water iz cold." Once again, I looked to the water. It was still still and apparently very cold. I slowly began to squeeze myself into the wet suit. It was the full body kind, the kind you see Shamu trainers at SeaWorld wearing. This particular one was fire-engine red. I remember wondering if sea monsters were colorblind.

Next, I was handed a pair of what they were calling "skis." I couldn't say if they were poorly made, but I could tell you when they were made, and that was well before I was born. They looked like a pair of two-by-fours covered in white house paint! The boots that were nailed onto them were so rotted and cracked that my right pinky toe was completely exposed. I was beginning to feel a little less confident in my decision. I looked out over the water. It was still, still still, perhaps even stiller. I waved to my friends on land and then slowly dipped into the water.

Cold. So very cold. I remember feeling like I had to swallow my kidneys down as they frantically tried to escape from my body. My toes curled up, my back tightened, and my heart stopped. Within seconds I was having trouble breathing and unable to blink. I looked down; I couldn't see my feet, my legs, my wiener space, or my hands! Where were my hands? The water was *black*. It was black-cold, and I couldn't see anything farther than six inches down! I quickly pulled the skis onto my feet and watched as the boat pulled away. The rope tightened as the vessel picked up speed. I grabbed the handle, bent my knees, and after a quick jolt I was up. Thumbs up from the boat. Thumbs up from the shore. I'm skiing! I was skiing on the mother-flippin' ocean! I swished right. I sloshed left. I. Was. Boss. And then it happened—I hit something.

My right ski dipped into the water and shattered, leaving nothing but the boot on my foot! I had time for a quick "oh shit" before spiraling headfirst into the water. With my ears ringing, I frantically gathered myself upright and located the boat. The same boat that had somehow yet to notice that the human they were towing had exploded off the rope. There was no use in screaming—they'd get around to me at some point—so I bobbed, quietly. In the ocean. Like a fire-engine-red buoy.

I don't know how long I was in that water. Maybe it was a minute; maybe it was a year. Either way, I knew I was not alone, because I felt a noise. It was weird, like I was standing next to a speaker while someone hummed into the microphone. I felt this: "Ooooooooommmmmmmmmm." It shook my organs. And then, "Ooooooooohhhhhhhh-Mmmmmmmmmmmmm," which made the water vibrate. I tucked my feet up into a ball and began to frantically swivel around looking for the source. I couldn't see anything! My friends on the shore seemed to have no interest in my plight at all, and the sounds were getting more intense. Suddenly, the water began to churn. I saw a quick flash of white and then, right there, less than three feet away, it surfaced. Cold dark eyes. Smooth black skin. The guttural sound of ocean water being pushed through its stupid little blowhole.

What were the odds? Insurmountable, a billion to one at best. I've spent half my entire life trying to avoid what is perhaps the most ridiculous fear a boy from the Midwest could have: *do not get eaten by a whale!* That was the goal.

A second beast surfaced to my left. Shit, someone's gonna have to call my mom and tell her that I was eaten by a large, uneducated, aquatic mammal. This is outrageous. I simply could not comprehend all the little things that led up to the very moment wherein I'm forced to live out my worst nightmare. A third came from directly beneath. Tears began to well up in my eyes when my bare skiless foot rubbed across the back of the rubbery beast. Now whether or not these behemoths had the ability to sense fear, I'm not sure. But I will tell you that if they had the ability to sense urine through a forty-year-old red wet suit, they hit the jackpot as I (not surprisingly) drained out a gallon of warm liquid shock.

In total, there might've been twelve. They were massive and unafraid. It was obvious by the way they ignored my whimpering pleas; these water devils feared no man. So like a big red cherry atop a tasty saltwater sundae, I merely waited to be consumed.

I don't remember getting into the boat, but eventually I was told that it was a school of "harmless" northern whale blah-blah-blahs that caused me to cry and urinate like a newborn. I found no solace in the assumption that they let me live. None of that mattered, because I was right. My fear, although ridiculous, was warranted. I lived it; it happened. It. Was. Real! Which means, the only thing worse than floating with flesh-shredding demon whales is the realization that somewhere out there, tirelessly searching is a white van with tinted windows…and it's looking for me.

Romancing the Stone

There's an old Chinese proverb I made up that states, "To not be startled when a panda sneezes will only precipitate the toothy shrill of a dragon forged in Satan's kiln." Not one to mince words or metaphors, but after staring at this clumpy sequence of words for the past hour, I finally understood what it meant. It's about having the fortuitous balance between what you expect to happen (nothing), and how well you handle pain when that nothing turns into an unforgiving demonic clown giggle as it makes its slow jagged journey from your kidneys to your bladder.

7:00 a.m., August 31, 2013. Chicago, Illinois

I knew something wasn't right the moment I woke up. I was feeling a bit…well, "umph-y," but all indications surrounding my sudden internal discomfort led me to believe it was the amazing plate of big-boy nachos I'd crafted for dinner the night before. Cathy, on the other hand, was convinced that my wincing was a not-so-original excuse to get out of a dry wedding later in the afternoon. I assured her my intentions were pure, and I warned her that a three-hour drive into rural Indiana seemed less than ideal. She rolled her eyes and told me to get dressed.

Roughly 9:00 a.m.

After driving hunched over the wheel for the previous hour, the sight (for the first time ever) of Gary, Indiana, brought on a sense of relief as the sharp pain that had been pestering my back suddenly disappeared. The feeling of "umph" was gone. "It must've been a cramp," I thought. "It was probably, mostly, just a cramp."

Wedding, 2:00 p.m.

"Do you?"
"I do."
"Do you?"
"I do."

Kiss. Hug. Pretzels. Punch. Congrats and good-bye.

5:00 p.m. Our family has decided that the eclectic menu of the local TGI Chili-Bees is the best option for curbing our appetites.

"Are you OK?" Cathy asked. "You're sweating!"

"I don't know. That cramp came back. I'll go walk it off." I made my way down the hall, past a palm tree, and into "Flavor Country." From there I slowly maneuvered around a pile of driftwood, a life-sized replica of Dale Earnhardt high-fiving a miniature wood carving of Bobby Knight, a cactus wearing a Purdue sombrero, seven and a half Bud Light Lime signs, and a map of Paraguay before I found the bathrooms. I stepped through the door labeled "Blokes."

I unbuttoned my shirt and loosened my tie before splashing a handful of cold water onto my face. I couldn't stop sweating, and my hands were becoming numb from an onslaught of quick shallow breaths. The pain was so unfamiliar, so alarming, that I began to fear an alien was about to announce all its Earth-annihilating intentions by shredding through my midsection. I hobbled back to our table, took a few sips of water, and latched onto Cath's hand. I gave her an eye-squinting explanation about the possibility of death. She took one last Chicken-Fried Buffalo-Jack-Stuffed Ranch-Burrito-Popper, dipped it into a pool of Jim Beam-Teriyaki-Peanut M&M sauce, and walked me to the car.

"What do you want to do? Do you want to go to the ER? It's about thirty miles away." She knew I based all decisions on financial gains and losses—hospital bills are a loss—but she was trying to make it seem as though I had an option...I don't. I told her I would be fine enough to go back to her brother's house and lie down. She placated me. She drove.

5:30-ish. We are slowly beginning to accelerate through countryside.

The intense pain suddenly shifted from unbearable to *holy shit!* The morbid sensation was similar to waiting for a partially chewed Dorito to slowly make its way down your chest, except you replace chest with lower back and Dorito to Lucifer's hedgehog. The little relief I got by planking was offset by the fact that my

12

butt was being clenched so hard I was afraid that the slightest fart would literally lacerate my tush.

"Cath?" I whined.

"Yes?"

"Maybe we should just stop at your brother's house so you can change out of your dress and take off your heels…then we'll talk about going to the ER?"

"Sure, babe."

Somewhere on a road, not at a hospital

Fifteen miles out, I took a turn for the worse. My steady breaths evolved into an all-out pant, and I've mastered the art of drooling. I was a frothy mess, and just as it seemed it couldn't get worse, I began a screaming confessional. After shocking Cathy with a number of unmentionable sins, I blacked out. When Cathy noticed she went right into your standard "violently shake the face of a passenger in your car if you notice they have passed out from pain, while keeping one hand on the wheel and both eyes on the road" method. This worked about as well as you'd think. I woke up screaming so loudly that she put the car into hyperdrive. Faster! Faster! Faster!

She tried to console me—"A couple more miles to the house"—but I was having none of it! I'd totally lost control of body and mind. I was convulsing and couldn't stop quoting the rules for taking care of a Mogwai, circa 1984's *Gremlins*: "Don't feed after midnight. No bright light. And never ever get them wet…Cathy, I love you, but please…Get. Me. To. The. ER!"

Hospital

We pulled right up to the door. I was soaked from head to toe and walked like I'd just been struck by lighting. They offered me a wheelchair, but I opted for the awkward hobble-skip-tiptoe-pee-pee dance walk into the exam room. Once I was strapped down, they gave me morphine…

Oh, morphine—morphine, morphine, morphine, let me tell you about morphine. Morphine is the most fantastical thing *ever*! It feels like you're swimming on a bed of stardust covered with seven-thousand-thread-count sheets. My veins were slowly being filled with an elixir I can only describe as blue cough drops and Altoids. I felt it traveling from my neck to my fingertips. It made me smile. I had a feeling; I felt the way James Franco looks. *It is woooooooooooooooonderful!*

With the pain now gone, it was time to fill in the all-important information pack. How they expected someone on a morphine drip to dole out any relevant information is and was beyond me, but Cath filled in the blanks. First, a nurse asked for my social, to which I replied with my zip code. When she told me I was "missing" a few numbers, I gave her the telephone number I had when I was six. When she said I was still "missing" two numbers, I added my address. Next, they asked a few questions about my family history. Apparently, I answered "My wife is hot" or "I am of Aboriginal decent" for all of them, and as Cathy would later recall, I kept repeating that I wasn't taking no for an answer. At some point they decided that I was info-useless, and they agreed it was best to send me for some tests.

When you're on morphine, it doesn't take much convincing to get you onto a bed with wheels, so I flopped down on a gurney and was happily whisked away into the ominous X-ray area. When the doors opened, two beautiful women rushed out to greet me, so…*aw, yeah* to me. Everything about this situation was dreamlike. I was feelin' fine, lookin' fine, and spinnin' tales. Somehow I had come to the conclusion that I was probably the coolest guy they were ever gonna x-ray. This egotistical dream and disturbing vision of self quickly turned into a nightmare when those Sirens in scrubs asked me to "drop trou."

Look, I'm not modest at *all*, and 99 out of 100 times on morphine, this wouldn't have been a problem, because 99 out of 100 times I would've been wearing some sort of "superhot docs want me to drop trou X-ray apparel." Unfortunately on that day I was not. You see, when I get dressed up, as I had done for this wedding, I like to wear my superhip, sorta-tighter-than-they-need-to-be cherry-red pants. The problem is, these pants only look good (and believe me they look good) if they are sans panty lines. In order to combat this fashion faux pas I wear these—oh God—baby-blue-fat-man-on-a-Brazilian beach-bikini-briefs, and they are supersnug, unnaturally so. Cathy thinks they are hysterically *awful*. She often admits to being embarrassed just knowing that I'm wearing them.

I tried to convince the technicians to put me in the machine headfirst, but they were pretty set on following procedure. Reluctantly, I tried to envision how this scenario would play out, and it did not look good. I found out quickly that nothing demoralizes a man more than being told to "pull your pants down around your ankles, but keep your shoes on." The thought of this made me queasy. I conceded and followed the directions, only to have the situation escalate into a full-blown panic when I attempted to stand. Inauspiciously, I'd come to realize that my legs wouldn't work, and my belt had become some sort of unsolvable puzzle—morphine! The ladies were forced to intervene, and within seconds, I was a confused and vulnerable ninety-year-old man. Cherry-red pants drooped around my vampire-white ankles, and the front of my collared shirt was tucked ridiculously into my little, itty-bitty, teeny unimaginably tight, baby-blue bikini briefs. Helpless I stood, in all my awkward glory, ready to shrivel up and die from embarrassment. But not before they each grabbed an arm and held me up as I shuffled my feet like a darling little penguin across the room and into the machine. I felt them shaking with laughter, and by the time the whole ordeal was over, I couldn't even look them in the eyes. I was broken. Minutes later a kidney stone was confirmed. We left with some prescriptions, and I waited three weeks for that little S.O.B. to exit into the toilet with a clink.

I often think back to that day and all the lunacy that surrounded it. I think about that newly married couple and pray their marriage lasts through all the trials and tribulations that are present in our everyday lives. I think about my own marriage and how much my love and affection toward Cathy was strengthened during a time of crisis; my wife is my eternal mate. But more importantly, I'm reminded of an old Greek adage I made up that states, "When the sour grapes fall from the branch of narcissism, only he who wears the little, itty-bitty, teeny, unimaginably tight, baby-blue bikini briefs shall taste its humility," or roughly translated, "A kidney stone is made worse when your underwear is ridiculous."

An Artificial Compromise

"But I've always had a real tree." Had I known that these seven little words would soon create a fear of evergreens and nearly cause my death, I would have never agreed. But I have trouble saying no, especially to her. I'd like to think that during normal circumstances I would have fought this tooth and nail, but it was our first Christmas as a married couple, and she was doing that pouty lip-biting thing I absolutely cannot resist. This sultry maneuver has a 100 percent success rate. It's the reason we have a stationary bike (which is so seldom used, I'm forced to call it functional art), go to movies starring Channing Tatum, and are currently wearing matching wool sweaters complete with embroidered reindeers. (In her defense, I get to pick out where we eat dinner, once she gives me my options.)

I don't do well with change. And growing up, a real tree was never an option; and by default, assembling an artificial tree had become a major part of my holiday experience. On the other hand, Cathy never had a fake tree. Her holiday experiences were based on the smell of real pine. Now that we're married, we must consider this quandary and agree on a solution that'll appease both parties. But it's never that easy. An amiable discussion can turn sour quickly. Nothing is ever etched in stone, and the slightest disagreement becomes a catalyst for enough verbal warfare and mind trickery, to quickly obliterate any thirty-year-old traditions. But in order for a marriage to work, all disputes have to end the same way. They must end with a compromise. For every god-awful romantic comedy she drags me to, she's more than willing to cozy up and watch some football. That's marriage, plain and simple. On that particular day, she won. We did what she wanted to do, the way she was used to doing it. We would get a real tree for Christmas, because that's how this marriage works.

I'm not gonna lie. I was excited by the idea of driving out to the country and chopping down an evergreen in its youth. I packed a tiny handsaw into the trunk, and with the temperature reading somewhere in the single digits, I assumed when she pulled into the Home Depot that we were getting special equipment, for precautionary measures. Cathy, a pro tree wrangler and ever the visionary, was probably thinking that for his first time out, "Jim should have a chainsaw." And frankly, I couldn't have agreed more. A finely tuned wood-searing, mulch-making weapon of coniferous destruction seemed both practical and efficient.

A one point in my life, I hated this store. You'd open the doors and the pungent odor of false hope and desperation saturated the air, and I wanted no part of that. I'd walk in, immediately seek out the patio furniture, and hunker down until whomever I was with found the stainless steel wing nuts they were looking for. Sitting comfortably in my makeshift backyard, I'd laugh as confused customers lingered from lumber to dirt. All had the same panicky look plastered to their faces. All the "do-it-yourselfers" stumbled from aisle to aisle looking for ways to fix the plumbing disaster they accidentally created because some how-to book said anyone with thumbs could save a few hundred bucks.

However, my disdain for this place changed the day we moved into our new house. Now I skip—that's right, skip—through the aisles giddy with anticipation and smugly ignoring those underachievers sitting on plastic wicker couches. Now I'm part of that collective smell, a shameful mix of sweat, failure, and Drakkar Noir (in that order), and I love it! I find a certain amount of satisfaction scouring the concrete floors for the tools and putty needed to temporarily mend the damages I accidentally created, because I too have thumbs.

Upon exiting the car, I started to sweat. My body began to quiver in anticipation of my new toy (oh, the things I intended to saw). The store's doors opened, and I took a big whiff. Smells…so…good. I was all set and headed down the aisle of cutting things when Cathy grabbed the back of my coat and pulled me onto a poorly lit, snow-slathered patio. At the time, I was certain the chills that ran up my spine were due to the inclement weather. Little did I know that evil was lurking.

I found myself standing in a graveyard, a place where good trees went to die, a chain-link oasis where pathetically dried-up twigs were bundled in equally pathetic plastic fishnet stockings. The whole scene was surreal. It saddened me to see these once great freestanding trees leaning wistfully against makeshift wooden pens, while customers were seduced by the surreal sounds of *A Very Hall & Oates Christmas*.

"What are we doing here?" I snapped.

"What do you mean?" she snapped back. "We're picking out our tree." Her tone suggested I was an idiot for asking.

"Here? In the parking lot? This is where we're getting our 'real' tree? They have price tags stapled to them!"

"Where did you think we were going? Did you think we were gonna drive out to the boondocks and chop one down?"

"Yes! That's exactly what I thought. I even filled a thermos with cocoa."

Seriously? Was I crazy to assume that since she grew up in rural Indiana, getting a Christmas tree was going to be an adventure? Am I delusional enough to think that our first real tree would be found while hiking into the unforgiving landscapes of a Jack London novel? How dare I think that we would trek up and down the dense and dangerous woodlands, quietly isolated by nothing more than our voices caroling off the shimmering snowdrifts. How dare I think our arctic journey would connect us on spiritual level. And, oh, how dare I think that together we'd be forced to fight off all the wicked elements of nature, meet our inner demons, punch Jack Frost in the face, and overcome starvation for a tree—our very special tree.

The tree was to be the perfect combination of wood, sap, and needles. A beacon of hope illuminated by the heavens above. An unfettered sanctuary where woodland animals come to pray and sacrifice other animals…or humans! A tree that provides shelter to those who stumble upon its majestic canopy and the only place on Earth where magic eagles come to nest. More importantly, it would be the one tree that defines the word Christmas itself…that's the kind of tree I wanted to saw through, tie to the roof of our car, and adorn with trendy Crate & Barrel ornaments. It is evident that what we had was a failure to communicate.

Defeated and demoralized, I moseyed through the stupid concrete forest trying to conjure up the Christmas spirit my wife was somehow glowing with. Everyone from the patio manager to Hall and Oates was jing-jing-a-linging with it—everyone but me. Did the decision to compromise my tradition of putting together an artificial tree cost me the ability to find joy? Or was it something else? I quickly figured out that if I didn't say anything for the rest of the day, there'd be a chance I could salvage my idea of Christmas. I took a deep breath, cracked my knuckles, and created some semblance of a smile. I decided to take one for the team, even if it went against everything I believed in.

"Now hold those two next to each other. OK, put the one on your right down and switch it for the one with the red tag. Nope, too short. How 'bout that one?"

This went on for about twenty minutes. I didn't say much; I just nodded, grinned, and continued to collect random samples of pine and squirrels to my sap-laden hands. At some point during the shuffling of trees, my hand became covered in feathers! We never actually saw a bird, but if I had to guess, somewhere perched in one of those dying trees was a terrified naked finch.

"That's it!" she exclaimed. "That's the one!"

I haphazardly agreed. She was oblivious to the fact that this was the sixth time she'd seen this tree. I didn't have the energy to explain how it wouldn't fit in Daley Plaza, let alone our living room. I just wanted to go home, but there was a matter of adornment to deal with. I knew we'd need somewhere in the vicinity of thirty thousand lights to trim this behemoth, so I left her to deal with the tree, and I escaped back into the store.

Once inside, I was led by unseen forces through the chasms of paint, light bulbs, door hinges, and caulk. When I finally stop, I find myself face-to-face with the BuzzKutter850Z, and she is magnificent. Running my fingers over her pristine laser-etched blade, patent-pending foam rubber no-slip grip, and automatic one-touch start button, a chill ran down my spine. It was destiny. For reasons I can't explain, I was brought to this very saw. Somehow we were connected; she needed me as much as I wanted her. She was hungry, and I was sad. It was obvious to me that the only way either of us would come to terms with our destiny would be to sneak her into the car and drive off on a beer-soaked, *Top Gun* soundtrack–blaring, testosterone-driven road trip to Canada. That's right—somewhere in the Yukon we'd pitch a tent, lip-synch to "Danger Zone," and singlehandedly carve a niche out of their precious ecosystem. Come hell or high water, I'd be back for her, and we'd have our day, but until then, I'd agree to take home a tree chopped down by the hands of Big Business USA. Good-bye, BuzzKutter 850Z. I love you.

"Would you like help tying it to your car?" I knew he was just doing his job, but this was the one part throughout this whole ordeal that would remain unchanged. I was the only one who would be tying a tree to the roof of my car—me! There was no way I was gonna let some eighteen-year-old chump in an oversized orange vest take this from me.

"No, I think I can handle it," I replied smugly, sending him back to collect more shopping carts. Then I—alone—lugged this redwood to the car.

"Do you think it's too big?" Cathy asked. I didn't answer because yes, it was too big. We hoisted it up on the roof, and I began to tie it down. I looked at her; she was happy and loving every second of this. How dare I stand here and quietly hate on her tradition! She didn't deserve that. Maybe real trees are better than their artificial counterparts, and to be fair, this really hadn't been that bad. The whole point of this trip was being together; the tree was really just a small part of the equation.

She waited patiently in the car while I methodically manipulated the twine up, over, through, and around the hearty pine branches. After a series of complicated knots, I felt confident that our tree, which was now trapped under a web of crisscrossed twists and braids, was securely fastened to the roof of our car. The only thing left to do was transport this evergreen across town to the house where it would stand as the epicenter of our holiday season.

"All set?" she chirped.

"Yup, it's all good." And it was, for the first couple miles. Contentedly, we drove down the street sweetly holding hands and alternating sips of cocoa out my sleek new Eddie Bauer thermos. I never saw the pothole.

"Careful!" she cried. What transpires over the next half mile is both tragic and miraculous. Whether it was the pothole, some rare form of karma, or (and I'll never believe it) poor knotsmanship on my part, the tree began to slide.

"Jim, the tree! Oh God, the tree!"

When I finally realized that it was in fact the tree sliding down over the windshield and not a prolonged blink that was blocking my view, I panicked. For some reason the part of my brain that's supposed to monitor common sense failed. Within seconds, I became an irrational lunatic on wheels and the reason for at least fifteen near-death experiences.

I screamed. She screamed. We both screamed. What I should've done was stop the car, but I was already hopped up on fear and adrenaline, and swerving was the best I could do. I successfully managed to bob and weave through three lanes of traffic for the better part of four blocks. Of course, the herky-jerky movements and high-pitched screaming did nothing to prevent the tree from its decent. So it came as no surprise when the bulk of the tree started careening down the windshield only to magically disappear under the front of the car as I ran it over. At this point we should have felt a sense of relief; after all, we were still alive, but…

Cathy noticed that the twine, which had followed the tree from the roof to the road, was not only still attached, but oddly taut. I had assumed that once the tree was off the car and had its taste of rubber, it was out of our lives forever. Little did I know, the tree was not as willing to part ways.

"Oh. My. God. The tree is still attached!" she yelled in a weird, whispery, talking-to-yourself kind of voice.

"What?"

"It's attached! The tree is still attached! We're dragging the tree! Oh my God, we're dragging the tree!" Well that explained all the honking, flashing lights, and middle fingers. I took a second to absorb her words before I peered into the side mirror. Sure enough, there it was, a good fifteen feet behind us, shedding pine needles and wagging like a happy dog's tail. We were officially a spectacle.

She pleaded with me to stop the car, but I couldn't, not in the middle of the street, not there in front of all those people. I'd be laughed at…or arrested. It was during these next five blocks of terror when the last remaining knot magically or perhaps purposefully untied itself from the roof of the car. We watched in relief and let out a collective sigh as the last bit of twine whipped down the front of the car. If it were alive, and I'm not sure that it wasn't, it would've winked as it passed out of sight, because only twine with a motive and malicious intent could concoct such an evil finale. Suddenly, and quite inexplicably, the devil twine looped itself around the driver's side mirror and, with relative ease, yanked it clear off.

"That's it!" I yelled. I couldn't take it anymore. I feared that if I didn't stop right there and then, we were definitely gonna die. I pumped the brakes, wiped away an unusual amount of sweat from my forehead, and stepped out onto the frozen concrete. After a quick prayer to the heavens, I surveyed the situation. Lying on the street behind the car was the broken mirror, which was still attached to the death rope, which was still attached to our filthy mangled Christmas tree. I was being punished. By whom or what I wasn't sure, but something somewhere was trying to run some serious interference. Did our Christmas tree traditions overlap, causing a tilt in universe? A tilt so rare it created a gravitational anomaly? A vortex of wind, fear, and inertia summoned to untie the one knot holding this whole day together? Although it was illogical and absurd, I concluded that it might in fact be possible.

After prying her fingernails from the dashboard, she reluctantly stepped out of the car and into the cold. We stared at the tree for quite some time, silently calculating the odds and trying to mentally break down the ridiculous chain of events that started the moment we took that curious turn into the Home Depot parking lot.

"Holy shit! No one is going to believe this. I mean, seriously, what the hell just happened?" I shook my head in disbelief, knowing full darn well she was right.

Other than the mirror being ripped off, the damage to the car was minimal. The hood was scratched clear down to the bumper, and something was leaking from underneath. If we hadn't been through so much, I would've just left the tree there, but I couldn't—it would have been a waste of eighty dollars. I untied the mirror, threw it into the backseat, and then retied what was left of our tree to the roof. Sad, shocked, slow, and silent is how we drove the rest of the way home.

Philosophically speaking, I learned a lot about marriage during that trip. I think I finally understood why I married Cathy. I married her 'cause I love her and all of her traditions. So she's a country girl who gets her Christmas trees at a hardware store—big deal. I once bought ground beef at a gas station. The fact of the matter is that although we were both scared and violently ill after both of these instances, we were still here—together. My Christmas spirit was not teetering on the blades of a chainsaw or stuffed in a big cardboard box. My Christmas spirit was sitting next to me screaming, "We could've died!"

Once we got home, we dragged the tree through the house, cleared some space in the living room, and we pushed the bald, flat side flush against the wall. It was ugly, a horrifying example of the holiday season almost too frightening to look at, but it was ours. We were afraid to decorate it with lights for fear that the lingering motor oil, which dripped from its trunk, would ignite and burn the house down. So we were forced to accept a collage of eerie shadows that the lunar light cast upon our living room. Like a bad piece of art or a prop from a Tim Burton movie, the tree provoked thought and discussion. For some, it even conjured up suppressed childhood memories. Not surprisingly, neither of us could stand to be left alone in the room with it. Although we now look back on this incident and laugh, it is important to know that neither of us blinked an eye when we purchased an artificial tree the following year. It was a decision based not on traditions, love, compromise, or even marriage; it was based on fear. The real tree almost killed us, and that was something we both agreed on.

Lucy and the Fly

We all want to be judged; it's in our genes. Everything we do is being "judged" by someone else—our bosses at work, our teachers at school, why it's even in the evil eyes of the monkeys at the Lincoln Park Zoo. We're always being evaluated; it's what helps us reach our own personal idea of perfection. For instance, Cathy judges the way I dress, and I (internally only) judge my wife's sense of style. I get a better understanding of what she thinks I should look like, and she gets to feel like she's helping me from being ridiculed. Needless to say, I never really cared a lot about what people thought of me. But that all changed the moment Lucy was born.

In one day I went from being judged as a reckless youth to being judged as a person whose sole responsibility is to keep a tiny human alive, healthy, and safe until I die. I would be judged…as a parent! I would be forever linked, evaluated, and ridiculed by friends, family, and passing strangers for every little decision I make, but more importantly, I'd be judged by Lucy. This little person's opinion of me is gonna matter.

Every step I take has to have a purpose; I have to be methodical.

I began to base all my newfound parental decisions largely on a dream that one day while accepting an Oscar, Grammy, Gold Medal, Emmy, or even a Tony, Lucy will look down at her prewritten acceptance speech and thank a very special man for all his love, support, and patience throughout the years.

"Without him, none of this would be possible," she'd say with a small crackle in her voice. The camera would pan to an attractive older gentleman sitting in the audience with his chest plumed out with pride and a tear welling up in his eye. He'd nod his head with approval; she would blow him a kiss and mouth the words "thank you."

Surprisingly, that handsome older fellow is Chase Todd, celebrity, action hero, and denture cream spokesperson. I, on the other hand, am sitting in a bar watching all of this unfold like Jon Voight watching Angelina Jolie accept a Golden Globe. That's right, somewhere during her first years of life I was judged and deemed not worthy, and because of that, some youthfully geriatric chump named Chase Todd gets my seat at the Oscars. This, of course, is not immediately true, and only a worst-case scenario.

My journey as a stay-at-home dad started six weeks after Lucy was born. Cathy went back to work, and I was left all alone with my small impressionable child. A crying, pooping, eating, sleeping, sleep-pooping, sleep-crying, poop-cry-sleeping, cry-pooping, cry-poop-crying, and—my personal favorite—"when did she eat chili?" child.

How boring it must be to eat nothing but white liquid all day. I feel as if I'm taunting her with my steak sandwich, extra blue cheese, sautéed mushrooms, and little brown bag of greasy fries. Damn this is good! I can't wait till she can eat solid foods, foods with color and flavor: red apples, red meats, red soda, red popsicles, and, oh sweet Jesus, red-filled doughnuts! Yup, she'd have to wait a few months before she could experience the flavor of red, but for now it's just plain ole white breast milk. Sorry, Lu, but I don't make the rules. I just follow the simply written caveman directions from your mom: Feed Lucy. Change Lucy. Lucy sleep. Repeat. This seemed simple enough.

Lucy and I had just begun to settle down for our third nap of the day, and everything to this point had gone according to plan until I was startled by the familiar sound of the impending summer months. Although I could not see it, I was completely aware that a not-so-common housefly was somewhere in the living room.

As most houseflies do, this one seemed to circle my head just as my eyes began to close. The buzzing was tremendously loud. I'd blindly estimated the size of this elusive insect to fit somewhere between a meatball and Mothra! Yet for some reason, I found it impossible to locate. The frantic beast sputtered and swooped with stealthlike precision, turning an irritating hum of anxiety into a steady white noise. Lucy's imperviousness became my comfort, and soon I became immune to it as well. I took one last glance around the room, and it was lights out. Boy oh boy, being a good dad was easy. My tired eyes began to close, and I started to nap.

It might have been a minute, might have been thirty, but suddenly I was jarred awake by a sound. A new sound…a different sound…a no sound. Gone were the acrobatics of flight that had been zipping around the living room. There was nothing, zilch! It was the unthunderous sound of silence that jolted me from my slumber.

Something was wrong. I shot up from the couch and surveyed the area until I focused in on a little black dot on the other side of the room. Bingo! I'd located the creature, and to my absolute horror, it had landed. It had landed nowhere near the uneaten crust of my steak sandwich nor on the corner of the television screen. No, that no-good, lazy, nonbuzzing menace had landed on Lucy's bottom lip, and he was huge!

She was dead asleep and a little more than ten feet away. My initial thought was to throw a pillow at it, but I couldn't take the chance of waking up Lucy. I'd have to go about this much more methodically. Then, just as I stood up, the fly disappeared, but it didn't fly away. In fact, the S.O.B. ducked inside Lucy's mouth. I froze. I was concerned that the slightest noise would compel the fly to zip down her throat and choke her from the inside. Worse yet, I didn't know how long I had been sleeping? Had this stealthy Oreo with wings already settled down with his family inside the belly of poor defenseless Lucy? Was she now doomed to unleash a new buzzing menace into this world every time we burped her? Cathy would have absolutely killed me if she knew that Lucy's first solid food was black, let alone a fly.

At this point it became a test of wills. Two forces on opposite sides of the law fighting over a young impressionable being. Star Wars! We were fighting for Leia! That's right—I was Obi-Wan and the fly was Vader (on a personal level, I would have much rather been Vader; but seeing as the fly was in black and I was wearing my wife's ridiculously comfortable white silk bathrobe, I had very little choice in the matter). His buzzing soon became the hard throaty breaths of evil. Lucy, an innocent and unknowing pawn of war, was incredibly still sound asleep.

"I see you in there," I whispered as he poked his dirty little head from out of her mouth.

"Buzz," he replied with a sense of sarcasm and downright snobbery.

"Get out. Get, get, get out," I whispered through my clenched teeth. As a side note, yelling at a fly does nothing. He was oblivious to the fight we're in.

What if Lucy woke up? What would she do? Would she breathe in and swallow it, or breathe out and send it cascading down her drool-soaked chin? I had to make a move. I took two slow steps and began closing in. I didn't know what was gonna happen when I got to her, but I had a feeling either Vader or I was going to die. Then without warning he appeared again. He crawled out of her mouth, over her nose, onto her eye, and finally to the top of her head. Then he began to do that disgusting, weird, leg-crossing bug dance all over her face.

I slowly raised my hand to attempt to an air slap, whoosh it off her head. I was hopeful I could gather enough wind speed to launch it into a closed window where it would crash and fall to its demise. On the other hand, it might have been big and strong enough to smash right through the panes of tempered glass, sending an explosion of shards everywhere, while stylistically recreating the infamous Death Star explosion.

Then she'd wake up to see me standing above her, covered in glass, wearing that ridiculously comfortable white silk robe, and I would be judged! She'd be disappointed by the lack of effort I used to rid her mouth of the fly. In five or so years, she'd verbalize this to her mother, who would tell our friends, who would tell their friends, and I would get picked up by the authorities. Lucy would of course persevere in the face of this tragic event to win her Oscar. Later she'd disown her father, and then out of spite, marry that Scumbag Chase Todd.

Then in an instant, the fly zoomed off her head straight up into the air.

What happened next appeared to be a death-defying reverse Blue Angels throw-triple-sow-cow barrel roll that ended with a laser-precise entrance right back into her mouth. It was like watching the *Millennium Falcon* dodge the errant lasers of an X-wing fighter. Unbelievable!

I stood there silently trying to revisualize what had just happened. No one would ever believe me, but what I'd just witnessed was the coolest buzzing thing ever! Then I felt the burning stare of confusion. She was awake! I wasn't looking at her, but I could feel those small impressionable eyes sizing me up for future ridicule. Finally, I drew my gaze down and looked her in the eyes. She was smiling! She was not judging me...well, maybe she was, but in my mind she was paralyzed with admiration and in awe of her statuesque father. Man, I must have looked like a Greek god standing there in that fantastic, fit like a dream, tickle skin, manhood murdering, so slippery smooth it makes you wanna pee every time you put it on, white silk bathrobe. Nope, there was no way she was judging me. She was giving me a look of acceptance. I was her means of support and comfort and she knew it. She knew I would never let anything happen to her, and, more importantly, she had no idea that she had eaten a fly. In her eyes, I'm a good father. And then...

She squinted her eyes, opened her mouth, and a left-for-dead, drool-drenched fly appeared. She'd been baiting me! She knew damn well that a fly had zipped into her mouth. She had set me up! Then Lucy gave me a look that I can only describe as "you suck." She pursed her lips together, leaving my exhausted little foe time for one last faint buzz, and then she swallowed. It was done. Lucy had eaten Vader.

I'm sure she did this on purpose. She was barely two months old, but she knew exactly what she was doing. She must have been sizing me up for weeks, waiting for an opportunity to flex her power and test my resolve. With one eye opened, she peered into my soul. I knew this was a crucial moment in our relationship; she knew what she did, and thus she had given me my first real task as a father. How I handled this particular event would inevitably shape our relationship. So what do I do? I do nothing. I feed. I change. We sleep. And repeat. In a few years, this tragic event will all be forgotten. It will cease to exist. And I know that because on the line in her baby book that asks what Lucy's first solid food was, I wrote bananas.

Raisin Ruby

What the…? What just happened? What is that? I jump to my feet and stick my finger in my nose. That was stupid. I shouldn't have done that. Uh-oh. My eyes are beginning to water. Panic sets in, and I'm finding it hard to breathe. Oh my God, should I call 911? "Ruby, what did you do? What did you stick in my nose?"

Sounds ridiculous, right? But that's what happened. We were playing on the floor, just kind of wrestling; I closed my eyes for one teeny-tiny second, and suddenly without provocation she decided to cram a small, yet-to-be-identified object into my nasal cavity. I wiped away a few tears and quickly surveyed the floor for potential culprits. Lego? Too big. Cheerio? Too crunchy. Ugh! Whatever it was, it was soft, small, and taking up residence next to my ocular nerve. Then out of the corner of my good eye, I saw something on the floor by the couch. They were small and dark. There were about fifty of them. I slithered down to all fours.

"Is that…? Could it be? Would she? Probably." I twitched my nose and let out an exasperated sigh. I'd identified the object. It was a raisin; Ruby had pushed a raisin up my nose.

It is one of those situations you can't really wrap your head around. A real WTF moment. Should I remain calm or worry? Calm seems like a logical solution, so of course I should worry, right? Yeah, I'm definitely gonna worry. I catch a slight second of composure and then breathe. I'm ready. Oh boy! Here. I. Go.

My pulse quickens, chest getting tighter, must relax. Oh, what to do, what to do, what to do? I run to the bathroom. I can hear Ruby's Godzilla-like footsteps slamming into the floor behind me. I'm scared. I get the uneasy feeling I'm being stalked. So methodical. Professional. She's quick like a ninja and stealthy like a dump truck. Her choice of weapon subtle and her attempt to suffocate me masterfully quick. I've underestimated the little girl; she's gonna be trouble. She lurches into the doorway. "Ah-ha dada!" I can see it in her eyes; she loves the panic she's instilled in me.

I stare into the mirror for a few seconds. How am I gonna get it out of there? I can barely see it! I mean its superstuck. I take a few steps back, place a finger to the left side of my nose, and blow. I expect the raisin to shoot out and shatter the mirror, but to my horror the only thing that becomes dislodged is my right eye from its socket. This is worse than I thought. I sit down on the side of the tub and try to regroup.

I'm dizzy. I'm sweaty. And I'm scared that if I accidentally snort too hard, this little juiceless grape will slam into my brain, causing instant paralysis or memory loss. What am I supposed to do? Do I go knock on the neighbor's door and politely ask if they would mind fishing a small piece of fruit out of my nose? I can't do that; they barely know me. Sure, I'd give them a story for the ages, but now's not the time. Plus, that's one of those favors you'll have to pay back tenfold. Something like, "Hey, you rememba dat time I dug in yo nose, pulled outta raisin, and saved yo life? Well, now I've come ta collect on dat favor. Take dis box ta Joey Knuckles on pier eighteen. Whadeva ya do, don't open it. Tellim my mudda said hello. Afta dat ya got two minutes beefa all hell breaks loose"—or something like that. I'm not talking it off the table; I just gotta go over a few more progressions before I go knock on that door.

I sit and stew on my options for a few more seconds. I'm about drive myself to the ER when Ruby comes charging past the door carrying a wooden spoon and kicking a head of lettuce. This did not shock me. Ever since Ruby figured out how to open the refrigerator door, we've been finding random pieces of produce in the weirdest places. At first I thought I was going crazy. I'd find myself asking questions like, "Did I put those baby carrots in my shoe?" or "Was I making a salad on the couch?" My personal favorite/nightmare came after lifting the toilet seat and finding two spears of asparagus floating in there. I just kept thinking that somebody really needed to chew her food better. Now I just get up and make sure that the door is closed.

On my way to the kitchen, I start to imagine what my life would be like if I had to live the rest of my life with this raisin in my nose. I've come to the horrible realization that I wouldn't make it a year. Seasonal sinus drainage would eventually be absorbed into the raisin, which would cause a slow swell. First it would morph into a grape, and then a prune, and then wham-crack! The pressure would split my skull into a million little fragments. Cause of death? Raisin. How humiliating.

Then it hit me. Ruby, was leading me to the kitchen. She had the cure all along! She, who stuffs the raisin in, also knows the raisin's out. It was a solution of cartoonish fruition—the pepper shaker! I had no time to wonder whether or not this was a terrible idea, but it seemed partially viable. The plan was to take a tiny palmful of pepper, quickly snort it into the unobstructed nostril, and wait to sneeze. The force of the sneeze should unleash the raisin from my head and effectively save me a trip to the ER or the docks.

Palm over nose, I snort—hard. The first thing I notice is the burning. It's extremely uncomfortable, and it feels like someone is sticking the business end of a cigarette up my nose. Next, the tears, followed by an awful and indescribable (burning shoes?) taste that adheres itself to the back of my throat. Finally, the sneezing. It begins with a simple "achoo!" Ruby thinks this is funny. One hundred forty-six brain smashing, neck-snapping, mind-erasing bursts of snot and wind follow this lone sneeze. Apparently, Ruby does not think these are as funny, because after every "oh God!" sneeze, I hear a blood-curdling cry of terror.

At some point during this fiasco, the raisin comes out. I have no idea where it went; I just know that it is no longer in my nose. In fact, based solely on the ferocity of my sneeze-a-thon, I wouldn't be surprised if upon exit, the raisin was going so fast it created a tear in the time-space continuum and is now floating somewhere in an alternate universe.

It takes less than a second from the time Cathy walks through the door to ask me why one of my nostrils is flaming red and the other was twice its usual size. I try to think of an excuse, something awesome that would stand up on its own merit and without further questioning, but I can't. Nothing I can say would make this seem less ridiculous. So I decide to tell her the only thing she'd believe. It's stupid and unbelievable, and eight hours prior I would have thought the whole thing was implausible, but it was the truth: "Ruby stuck a raisin in my nose."

That Time at the Grocery Store

Location: Jewel, Lincoln Avenue, Chicago
Date: For legal purposes I'd rather not say.

Upon entering the doors, I promise Lucy we can get one of those stupid big grocery carts with a car attached to it. She picks out a nice-looking red one, and I buckle her into the driver's side. Ducky, her stuffed sidekick, gets to roll shotgun, while Ruby, who is still too small for the car, gets buckled into the wire basket facing me. Both girls seem happy, so happy that I spend extra time in the produce. The horn is beeping, the girls are laughing, and I am killin' it! I'm having a slight problem steering this beast, but that frustration is offset by the amount of check marks flying off my list. We grab some ham at the deli, take a left through the bread aisle, and then assume a whimsical gait through coffee and cereal. Before you know it, our cart is pretty full, and I'm starting to feel an unbelievable sense of parental competency.

I'll admit, earlier I was a bit leery about taking this trip without backup. I've been in stores where screaming kids are being pulled through the aisles like rabid animals. I've seen what can happen when even the most well-behaved kid doesn't get the brightly colored cereal box she somehow feels entitled to. Sometimes, the lack of parental control is astounding! Inevitably, the teary-eyed spawn of Count Chocula gets her way, and I tsk-tsk-tsk all the way home. An outburst like that would never happen with my kids. As it is, my kids are doing great! In fact, the longer I shop, the more confident I become that this will be an incident-free trip. And then I hear—rather feel—what sounds like a drain unclogging.

I stop for a moment and pray that I am standing on a fault line. Maybe what I felt was a small seismic shift in the Earth's crust? I wait a few seconds, focus on the horizon to make sure the shelves are not swaying, before I slowly resume shopping. I don't make it more than three steps when something like a "burgaloop-blup-blup-blup..." begins to emanate from my body.

I halt. Immediately. My hands are gripped so tightly around the chipped plastic steering bar of the grocery cart that they begin to throb. I'm scared. This is *not* the sound or sensation of a casual fart; this is the beginning of a storm! Suddenly, I feel the weight of an intestinal plumbing problem muscle its way south of my belt. It is here—now! Smothered in a stagnant fog of bodily betrayal, I realize two things: an unfortunate grocery store incident is about to occur, and it has nothing to do with my kids.

I begin to gingerly step past the canned goods when I realize this is gonna be one of those life-changing moments. At the end of the day, I'll either be a "born again" Christian, or a card-carrying atheist. I need to find the bathroom, and I need to find it yesterday!

I want you to understand something. With one child, a trip to a public bathroom can be an unsettling chore, but with two? Act. Of. God! I'm only ten feet from where this whole thing started, and again I've stopped walking. I need to relax and control my breathing. Slowly, I begin to drag deep breaths through my nose and out my mouth. My concentration is monk-like. I'm staring down a box of penne pasta like it's about to blink. Sweat is beginning to bead across my forehead and drip over my eyelids. Seconds later, I begin channeling the four-year-old memories of a birthing class, and suddenly I'm going full Lamaze:

"Who-ha. Who-he…" It's dizzying. Colors are melting off boxes, and faces are appearing in the floor around me! I feel like I can bend steel, yet for some reason I can't stop the pressure that continues to build from inside.

Confused by the amount of time spent standing still, Lucy asks why we are stopped in front of the soups, but I don't answer. I can't—I'm about to break. My mouth begins to sweat, and gradually I lift myself onto my tippy-toes. Oh boy, I'm done trying; I'm not breathing this one off. Dammit! This is happening. This. Is. Going. Down! I am at DEFCON 9, the sirens are blaring, and my whole body is starting to convulse. I need to move.

Now I've lived a good life, seen a lot of things, and been a lot of places. I've witnessed evil deeds and have had my faith in humanity restored on more than one occasion, so I know a thing or two. But rest assured, one thing you can always bet on is no one—*no one*—has ever casually used a grocery store bathroom. They are there for emergencies only, like when you are 100 percent positive you will not make it home. Nothing good will come of this. Nothing.

Lucy peers her head out of the driver's side window: "Daddy? Are you OK?" My eyes are watering so badly, I can barely see her. "Hold on," I whisper. I gather all my strength and push—hard! After a second or two, the big red menace hauling two kids, a stuffed duck, and a week's worth of groceries has successfully achieved the impossible speed where all individual items are blended into a cosmic stream of random colors. Like the *Millennium Falcon* hitting hyperdrive, we're moving at the speed of light! As our skin begins to peel away from our bones, I'm not sure what's scarier: the fact that I am breaking the laws of physics, or the possibility that even light-speed will not get me to the bathroom quickly enough. Ruby is crying. Lucy is laughing. Both are out of fear. Lucy grips the little car's roof, and as I turn left toward the bathrooms, "Ping-BAM!" The driver's side wheel buckles under the cart and begins to gouge up the rubber flooring. Now the girls appear to be screaming, yet somehow neither is able to produce a sound; fear has frozen their eyes and mouths open.

I'm having that running-in-your-dreams sensation where every step only seems to get us farther from our goal. I drag the cart, kids, and groceries sideways past the cashiers. No one seems overly concerned, but someone in a green vest is dangerously close to saying, "Umm...Hazmat cleanup kit required in aisle eight."

I "park" the cart next to the ice cream cones. I unbuckle Lucy, who has a death grip on her duck, and in one motion swoop Ruby and the diaper bag under my arm (the diaper bag gives others the impression that one of the kids has had an "accident"). I see the door but don't even think to knock; I'm going on instinct, and instinct tells me that a flying jump kick a la Chuck Norris is in order. My foot meets the door, which nearly comes off the hinges. In one subtle move I land, pirouette, and quickly lock the door behind us. When I turn around, I realize we're in the Xanadu of public restrooms. It. Was. Huge! It had all the essentials: toilet, sink, trash can, and changing table. It also had enough room for a Toyota Prius, futon, vending machine, and a ficus tree. But I had no time to admire. I came here to do one thing and one thing only...dispose.

"Lucy!" I scream. "Stand in the corner. Don't touch anything!" The proximity to my relief seat now has my body doing an involuntary dance of spastic gyrations. I've inadvertently Zumba-d myself into a glossy wet shell of a man. It's as if gravity itself has

55

decided that it was gonna try extra hard to push my insides out through orifice number two. With Lucy frozen to the corner, I focus my attention on Ruby. What the hell was I gonna do with her…hold her on my lap? For reasons beyond my control, I begin to cry. I decide that the best course of action is to strap her onto the changing table (which is so conveniently located on the other side of this ridiculously large bathroom) and pray. I pray for the safety of my girls, and pray that no one, not one soul outside this room, can hear what's about to go down. Little did I know this cavernous bathroom and its wall-to-wall tiles would have a diabolical effect.

What transpires next is somewhat of a blur. Everything is so fast and loud. Ruby, strapped on the table, is screaming so hard that her belly button is about to transform itself from an innie to an outtie. Lucy is on the far side of the room marching back and forth, clapping and screaming the word *echo*, while I slowly dehydrate. Just as I'm about to reach the great white light, a garbled sound from beyond pulls me back to the present.

"Is everything OK?" said a shy yet concerned voice through the hollow door.

"Ummm…yeah. We've just had a little accident, no worries, be done in a second." I'm horrified to think that our calamity has disturbed the store so much, that management has sent some poor unsuspecting food bagger to make sure I wasn't slaughtering goats or performing an exorcism in their gigantic porcelain palace.

Ruby is growing a shade closer to blue and clearly hyperventilating. Lucy is still yelling the word *echo,* only now with her hands over her ears, she suddenly screams, "Daddy there is some poopie from your butt on your shoe!" I immediately assume this statement to be impossible, so I halfheartedly giggle it off, until I look at my shoe—sure enough, poopie.

It's hard to say exactly where this poopie came from, or if it was simply a poopie imposter, but it defies all logic that the poopie in question is in fact from my butt. Rather, I lean toward a magic bullet theory. This is clearly the work of Ruby. She must've been crying so hard it shot through her shorts, over the trash can, and onto my shoe, like some sort of CIA operation. Years from now the Jewel security team will be going over this like the Zapruder film.

Finally, with one last gurgle and a pathetic wet fart, it's over. I pull myself together, splash some cold water on my face, and make sure there's not an ode to Jackson Pollock anywhere in this room. I find a piece of candy at the bottom of the diaper bag and stick it in my mouth. I console the kids, who are now staring at me in either fear or astonishment. I spray out all the contents of the courtesy air freshener and slowly open the door. Once the Lysol cloud of shame has dissipated, I realize they were looking—they were all looking.

I nonchalantly hide my embarrassment in what I think is a playful quip: "Boy she *did not* like getting her diaper changed!" I say this to no one in particular; I'm just throwing it out there. Then Lucy screams to no one in particular, "No, Daddy *you* had a lot of stinky poopies in *your* butt! Not Ruby! Remember? *You* had a poopie on *your* shoe…it was disgusting!" I smile at her annoyingly loud correction, and then I pat the little truth-teller right on her honest little head. Out of the corner of my eye I see an employee open the door to the restroom and stare in awe. I not sure of the exact damage, but I wasn't gonna stay around to find out. With the diaper bag hanging around my shoulder and Ruby clutching onto my hip, I grab Lucy by the hand, and we leave. We walk

right out the door, leaving our groceries sitting in that
big red broken-down jalopy next to the ice cream
condiments.

Not a single word or sound is uttered as we get
in the car. Ruby is asleep even before we leave the
parking lot. Lucy appears to be consoling her duck. I, on
the other hand, drive; I drive all the way to the Jewel on
Western Avenue, because we still needed groceries.

The Cool

"Lucy, why did you grab that man's hand?" She's three, she gets confused, but this, this felt different. There was a calm to her approach, and it weirded me out.

"Daddy, I thought it was you," she said meekly.

"What do you mean, you thought it was me?" It had to be the shorts. It was the only possible explanation, and even that was a stretch.

"He looks like you."

I stand up from my crouch and stare at the man who's carefully showing his son the monkey bars. I tilt my head left then right. I look back to Lucy. "You thought *he* looked like *me*?" She nods. "That guy, right there?" I'm pointing to the only other guy in the park, and she nods again. I'm confused. This man doesn't resemble me at all. He's a mess! Wool socks, flip-flops, and a faded yellow polo shirt, which is just a visual appetizer to his oversized cardigan and backward Packers cap. His shorts? Well, they're nice. I'd wear them. Other than that, he looks like a cartoon! Yet she thinks *he* looks like *me*? After a pause, I suddenly realize what's happening. A panic builds, my palms begin to glisten with sweat, and the playground begins to spin. This is not about a stranger, or how he looks; it's the comfort he represents, and in just a few seconds, my life will change.

From a very early age, "cool" had eluded and attached itself to anything and everything that wasn't Jim Noonan. Once, in high school, I was told that I looked just like "that dude from *Ferris Bueller's Day Off.*" I remember saying, "Yeah, I can see that." I remember the feeling of swagger that washed over me as I began to imitate Ferris…the look I gave to those little glassy-eyed students as I began the first bars of "Twist and Shout." I was exuding the power and strength of Mr. All-American Dreamboat Cool Guy, and if they were having any doubts about my newly knighted status, I was about to unleash a rendition of "Danke Schoen" that was gonna make me a god. And then, "No, no, no, not Ferris," they said. "The other dude, his friend Cameron." Yup, I was Ferris all right: smooth, smart, and suave. I could totally see the resem—

Wait! What? Cameron? Oh, no, no, I'm a Ferris! Cameron looks…he's just…well, he's not…cool. But it was too late. I looked around and realized I had mistaken those glassy eyes of sympathy for admiration.

It took me years to get over that public shaming. But I persevered. Eventually, my outer Cameron became too powerful, and he beat my inner Ferris along with any delusions of grandeur right outta me. Then one day, the guy who played Cameron aged just enough to nullify our likenesses. Just like that, I was unceremoniously relieved of my duties as his fuddy-duddy doppelganger, and for three whole hours, I began to think that my life was moving in a much cooler direction.

But life had different plans. As I walked down the street, a nice young lady stopped, stared, and yelled, "Oh my God, you look just like Joey Fatone!" I gave her a flat broken smile, the one that only appears when your insides are crushed by the realization you're a dead ringer for the old guy from the little boy band N'SYNC. I literally would've taken any other band member as a compliment, but Joey?

This uncanny recognition went on for years until Justin Timberlake got wise, ditched his mates, and became an international megastar. Joey and the other three were never heard from again, and my coollessness streak ended at sixteen years.

For the first time in my life, I was free of monikers and unfortunate adjectives. I felt naked, scared, and alone. But I was eager to fulfill my destiny, so I went looking for cool. It was a long journey filled with personal growth and absurd inner monologues (if you take away a zebra's stripes, what color is it?). I spent weeks, months even, clawing—starving—for the accolades that come with being cool, but I couldn't find them anywhere. I walked, and I waited. With no sense of self, I looked under bridges and over rooftops, underwater and in shoe shops. I tried fakin' it, but it left a fraudulent taste in my mouth. I'd almost given up until Lucy came along.

As soon as she was old enough to use the word, I became the definition. Everything I did was "cool." Driving, dressing, eating with a fork…there were no limits! For the first time in my entire life, I was twenty-four-hours-a-day cool. Eat that, Fatone! My ego was growing daily, my complexion was clearer, and my seasonal allergies had disappeared. I was living the life I'd always dreamed of. I put everything I had into that word, that idea, that feeling, but as great as my life was, cool is impossible to sustain.

So here we are. I look over at the cartoon man, his son giggling, as they play deep into the afternoon sun. The boy watches as his dad tightens his grip around the warm metal of the monkey bars and swings from one to another: "Cool, Dad."

I watch it all happen. I feel it leave; it only takes a second. Cool found a new host, and he'll quickly transform this safe and unassuming man into an unstoppable force. He came down off the monkey bars taller, stronger, and filled with the admiration of a boy looking at a real-life superhero. Holding onto cool will test his limits and delve into the deepest parts of his soul. And in time, he'll realize cool doesn't stay around forever.

I grab Lucy's hand and begin a humbling walk home. I'm fine with "safe"; it's an outcome I accept and will not fight to alter. With that in mind, I turn and wave to the cartoon man. He returns the gesture, but he's hesitant. I'm sure he is thinking, "Who was that nerd?"

The Bigger Picture

"You only want to do what you wanna do. You're not seeing the bigger picture." That little phrase would come up more than once in the next few hours. "You can't just sit around on the weekends and watch football; we have to do family things." To this point, I have no argument. We should do more "family things." I just don't think becoming a member of Costco at 1:00 p.m. on a Sunday is one of the twenty million choices I would put in that category. The parking is terrible, and the lines will be twenty deep!

"Why can't I just go and do it on Tuesday?" I begin to plea as tears well up in my eyes.

"Because we should go as a family. Why can't we just go as a family? Did you read that article I sent you about 'Happy Families'? You didn't read it, did you? You need to read it, and we are going to Costco." She storms off shaking her head like I'm the most irrational person on Earth. Part of me suspects that she's trying to send me into a heart-flopping panic attack, one that can only be cured by purchasing a half-gallon drum of lavender body lotion.

Truth be told, this is not our first Costco membership dance. I often find myself arguing against family shopping at a place that uses a forklift to rearrange shelves. The truth of the matter is, that unless you're planning on spending a month away from civilization, you don't need a sleeping bag full of oatmeal. Until this very moment, I've successfully thwarted this tango many times, but this time it's different. I'll cave. I've played all my chips, and my lip-biting white flag is about to lead to the most ridiculous reason for becoming a Costco member: salmon. I know, I *know*—the only reason we are about to pay for a membership is because of this farm-raised menace to the pocketbook. Anytime we eat it, pass it, or think of it, Cathy mentions how much cheaper it'll be at Costco. Salmon is literally her whole argument for joining Costco, and after three years of arguing, it appears that she's finally gonna make it happen.

On the way there, I do my best to relax and go with the flow, but the tension is palpable. The morale inside the car was already low, and I can feel the wheels about to come off when I snidely tell the girls we are embarking on a "family fun trip." Cathy has had it with my attitude and looks at me with those "why'd I marry you" eyes. I quickly grab her hand and make a truce not to ruin our "special fun family adventure." She hates me.

Once we get there she's surprised—like for real surprised that we are jammed into a parking lot full of bird-flippin', horn-honkin' dummies. For the next thirty minutes we troll up and down this endless M. C. Escher-esque parking lot until we find a nice quiet parking spot, approximately 791 yards away from the entrance. When I ask Cath if she would like me to call a cab, she huffs and begins the twenty-two-minute walk to Salmon City.

At the door, I'm nearly tackled to the floor because I didn't flash the proper credentials. A spry older man named Mark puffs his chest, eyes me up and down, and then explains to me the code of conduct/policy/membership rules. I assure him that we mean no disrespect and that we are there to become members of this great bulk-buying society. He pats me on the back and leads me through some secret Freemason handshake before showing us to customer service. I must say that I'm impressed with their security measures. What are they hiding in there?

I wait in line nervously, very close to a panic. I watch as a steady stream of people exit the building with boxes full of boxes full of food that will go bad well before they are ever able to consume it. The lady getting our information asks if we would like to become "Executive Members." I assure her we are only here to buy salmon and that the "Regular Members" plan is sufficient. She smiles and says that Executive Members receive benefits like points and money throughout the year and that the salmon and other stuff will basically pay for itself. Cathy thinks this is worth it, and we are now officially Executive Members (let it be known there is no special bathroom for Executive Members, which irritates me to no end). We leave through the exit and whip around to the entrance where I flash my fancy black card at Mark; he gives me a fist pump, and I acknowledge with a salute. Then I proceed to crash into a refrigerator-sized box of granola bars.

For the next hour we methodically go up and down every aisle debating the needs of our household. Cath is continually wondering aloud whether "that's a good price for this?" My answer is always, "No." She says I need to see the bigger picture and then proceeds to dump a fourteen-pound box of arugula into our cart. My eyes widen, and assuming that we will now be eating salad every day for the rest of our lives, I toss in a three-gallon bucket of ranch dressing; she pulls it out and tells me to stop being such an "ass."

We are a happy family right up until we step into the frozen-food aisle. Here we begin to argue about the idea that "we can just put it in the freezer." To which I respond in various ways like, "It's not safe to have that much chicken/rice/waffles/cheese in the house." She huffs off and returns with a beautiful prehistoric-sized slab of salmon and gently places it in our cart. To ensure there is no damage to our membership-sealing monster, we put forty-eight rolls of paper towels on top of it. A purchase, we both agree is a smart buy, although neither of us have a clue as to where we will store them when we get home.

Lucy and Ruby eat every sample we pass. One of which, absurd as it sounds, is Cheerios. We've all eaten Cheerios, but apparently if you put six of them in a little white paper cup and hand them out for free, people go apeshit. Everyone is plopping big yellow boxes of the world's most popular cereal in their carts like they're fifty-dollar flat-screen TVs!

We finally make our way to the aisles that house the gorilla-sized tubes of toothpaste and drums full of enough Herbal Essences to clean the Canadian contingency of Sasquatches. Cath coyly puts a twelve-pack of deodorant into the cart. This blows my mind, and I lose it. Once again she says, "You're not seeing the bigger picture" and tells me it's cheaper to buy these here and store them at home until they are needed. I calmly explode, telling her that unless we are opening a Walmart or plan on selling them out of the back of our car, this is a ridiculous buy.

"Where are we gonna put them, and more importantly, how much deodorant are you applying every morning that makes this one of the few things we need in our cart?" After calmly discussing the merits of this purchase for a few minutes, we come to the gentle understanding that buying one or maybe two deodorants at a time when they are on sale is a much better option.

We get in line, pay, and finish our daily calorie burn as we walk the mile back to our car. The kids are in the backseat sharing an enormously gross Costco sundae. Cath has ripped open a pillow-sized bag of Cheetos and for some reason. I'm at peace. I'm calm. I lock my fingers between Cath's, kiss the back of her hand, and begin to think about what she said; "the bigger picture." What is it? Is this it? Was joining Costco a metaphor? Maybe it made our marriage a little tighter, stronger, warmer. Whatever it did, I feel alive.

We pull out of the parking lot and into the evening traffic. The sun is reflecting off the snow in a way that makes me think a higher force was at work today. Maybe I owe Costco my marriage and for that it should be thanked or at least properly recognized. I turn to look back, but I can no longer see it. I can't see a damn thing, because there are a bunch of big-ass boxes full of boxes full of food that we'll never eat before it goes bad crammed to the ceiling and blocking every flippin' view in the car.

Surviving the Apocalypse on a Budget

(This story was written during a time when the outcome of civilization was uncertain.)

"That's your reasoning? Zombies? Seriously? I think she thought you were serious." Cathy furiously whispers through her clenched teeth as the membership representative leaves the room. All these years and I'm still amazed that Cathy is still amazed at what comes out of my mouth.

"I was serious! You think I'm joining this gym 'cause my cholesterol's high and I'm self-conscious about my calves? No. In fact, I'm sure I was a breath of fresh air. Bet she gets four, maybe five people a day coming into her office, giving her a story about how they used to work out but had to stop because they blew out their knee and became addicted to caramel-covered custard balls. Eh, that's bull. No excuses, no lies. If I'm doing this, I need motivation and purpose. Think about it. Zombies, they don't tire."

"Quit being so dramatic. I don't know why you had to make us look like a couple of weirdos. You could've just said that we want to lose weight."

"Please. Everybody in here wants to lose two pounds this and ten pounds that. When, and if, it comes time for the zombies to walk and this world to end, who do you want on your team? The guy who joined the gym to master Zumba? Or me…the guy who'll be able to run pretty fast while holding a five-pound kettlebell over his head?" She rolls her eyes in disgust, but somewhere deep down inside, she knows I have a point.

We leave the building, and I pop a lean against the nearest wall. This whole process has been much more liberating and exhilarating than even I could've imagined. I was hesitant about spending that kind of money on something so…so unfulfilling? But now— now my brow is beading with sweat. Sharp pains and sudden bursts of adrenaline cause me to haunch over. Instinctively, I begin to pull long slow streams of air in through my nose. Wide-eyed, I notice Cathy slowly trying to distance herself from the man she married. The man she loves. The man who just openly admitted his reason for joining the gym was to be more physically prepared for the impending zombie apocalypse.

Cathy was buzzing with irritation and embarrassment, so I was pretty much ignored for the rest of the day. She hates it when I talk about the end of the world, but not nearly as much as I hate it when she talks about that god-awful NBC drama *Parenthood.* "It's sooo realistic," she'll sigh. Um, barf? The last time Craig T. Nelson acted anywhere near the vicinity of "realistic" was *Poltergeist* (that is an undeniable fact).

Anyway, I'll admit, the combination of those stupid Mayan prophecies and that sphincter-clinching show *The Walking Dead* has had me on pins and needles for the last eighteen months! And it's not because I believe there's a slight chance that a Guatemala-sized meteor is gonna slam into the heart of old mother Earth causing a long sweeping hammer of pestilence and tainted water that will quickly manifest itself into a wrathful dance of epic destruction and the complete and utter annihilation of the human race (breath) 'cause I don't think about that at all. Nope, my fears are strictly financial…and of course zombies.

So here we are. Potentially ten months away from a good-bye five thousand years in the making and

Cathy has suddenly mistaken my credible sensibilities and empirical way of thinking for lunacy.

Do we really need to spend money on long-term items and investments when there's a possibility we'll not be around long enough to reap the full benefits and obtain the satisfaction needed to enjoy said purchase? I think not. Hence, I've created the Armageddon budget, and it's flawless-ish. I suggested that from now until December 21, 2012, we take the money we should spend on sensible long-term items such as a new mattress, stove, and rugs and spend it on awesome things like rare spicy cheeses, glow sticks, and flan. Sure, a house would be a nice investment, but why in the world would I want to spend the next couple years fixing up a place if there's a chance that Earth will swallow up all my hard work? I'd rather have cupcakes or a meat grinder.

So that's it, that's the plan. Hold off on any "big ticket" items until we wake up on the morning of December 22, 2012. It is only then, after we realize that our Earth is whole and the dead continue to sleep peacefully that we will begin to heal and correct our wicked ways. Once again, we learn to love and begin to mend our planet. We'll gather together with friends and family to tell stories about silly Mayan calendars. We'll shake hands, hug, and giggle at the thought of zombies eating our brains. Oh, how absurd it will all sound. And then, just as we're getting all comfy-cozy with our place in the universe, we'll look up to the heavens and wish upon a brilliant shooting star. Immediately after that, there'll be another, and then another and another. The night sky will glow with beauty as we stare in awe and thank God for the splendor he's bestowed upon us.

That is, until we realize that Earth is being assaulted from above by a bunch of crazy-ass aliens firing all their badass laser shooters and sucking up a stunned population for the purpose of harvesting our organs to power their intergalactic war machines. The End.

Curb Your Yeti!

"Daddy, what is that?" The tremble in her voice catches me off guard but sets the scene perfectly. I have no idea what it is, but I do know it wasn't there when we left.

"I'm not sure," I reply. We are still four houses away from our front door, but it isn't hard to notice the mass on our front lawn. I squint, but I can't make heads or tails of it. After I safely eliminate dog, cat, gopher, tiger, broken stork, ottoman, and melted tire from the list of suspects, I'm left to believe its either an aboriginal termite hill or Kardashian.

"Why isn't it moving?" Lu asks.

"I don't know. Maybe it's eating or planning an attack." I don't know what to do, but I'm sure whatever that thing is, it's loaded with rabies. There is no way we're gonna approach this thing blind, so I grab a rock and take aim. Soaring through the air, it flies a good fifty yards and lands within a foot of the beast. It doesn't move. Hmmmm. Perhaps it's Russian?

"Well, let's just start walking. Maybe it will scurry away as we get closer." Lu flanks me to the left. I arm Ruby, who is strapped into the stroller, with a stick. She's a tough one—battle tested, perhaps a reincarnated warrior princess. She immediately begins gnawing her weapon down to a fine point. Together we can do this. The wind picks up and the smell of death haunts the air. The pungent odor only intensifies as we creep closer to the mystery beast. Death turns to fear, fear turns to sadness, and sadness smells like...poo?

I wouldn't have believed it myself if I hadn't been there. It was two feet, if it was an inch! Shocked into a state of disbelief, I pull my shirt collar above my nose. Ruby begins to howl in fright; apparently there are things even a reincarnated warrior cannot comprehend. I turn the stroller away from the grisly scene and allow her older sister to comfort her. How is this possible? Is this the beginning of the end? What does it mean? What does it *all* mean? I look back to the corner. A few moments ago we stood there—happy—we were happy. We were—

"Da, who did that? Who pooped in our yard?"

I stumble for words, because I don't think it's a question of "who," but rather a question of "what." I have seen things, awful things, but this? This was the most colossal pile of dump *ever!* Seriously, six minutes and fifty feet ago I thought we were looking at a footstool! How can this be? We don't live in the Serengeti; this is one of the most recognizable neighborhoods in Chicago. Lucy has pushed her sister into the neighbor's yard, where they point to the corner and share memories of simpler times. I, on the other hand, am flummoxed.

My fixation is broken when Lucy screams, "Aren't people supposed to pick up their dog poop?"

I nod, explaining to her the rules of society: "Yes. If you have a dog and it poops, then you should pick up after it." But at this point, I don't have the confidence to say that this heaping dune of excrement was made from any dog in this realm. In my estimation, it is far more likely that this Earth-tilting mound of turd came from a rhino, T. rex, or—more plausible—a yeti, and if that's the case, I have no idea what the poop-removal etiquette is.

I contemplate my next move. Do I call 911, forestry, or Department of Defense? Is this a crime, vandalism, or germ warfare? Does the city have a poop-removal truck it sends out in extreme cases? These all seem like utopian options, but the fact of the matter is that I'm gonna have to take care of this. Not for me, but for the sake of all humanity. I wait not for the Archangel Gabriel and his words of God. For *I* am the "Chosen One."

I head to the garage for supplies. I grab a snow shovel, two empty garbage bags, gloves, the hose, and a bike helmet. I return to the front of the yard prepared for extraction. I make Lucy and Ruby watch; they need to know how far I'm willing to go to assure the safety of a normal life. My initial stab of the shovel collapses the western embankment of the structure to reveal what is very clearly a small sock—as in whatever made this must've eaten a foot! I jump back in horror. Am I on camera? Is this a joke? I listen for hidden laughter and wait for Mario Lopez to jump out of the bushes and tell me that I'm a new hidden-camera show. But the air is still. I move back in and begin the excavation.

The process takes way longer than expected. Somehow in less than an hour's time, the malicious entity begins to take root into the ground. For precautionary reasons, I'm compelled to dig up three square feet of soil. After bagging the final eight pounds and disposing of all potential evidence of an unknown urban gorilla, I step back and assess the damage. Scientifically speaking, I'm certain that this will either be the most fertile patch of land Chicago has ever seen, or one that has been so severely damaged that plant life will cease to grow there for a million years.

It's now lunchtime, and neither the girls nor I have spoken. As I put them down for their naps, I reassure them there is good in this world. They look at me with glassy eyes; they are much too young to comprehend the effect this day will have on me. I kiss their foreheads and fill them with a few good thoughts, but I know a restless slumber is in the works.

After an impurity-rinsing shower of *Silkwood* proportions, I try to put the day's events into perspective. Was it a careless oversight or the beginning of a more sinister plot? I look out the window, and all I see is the tattered landscape of a society on the verge of a emotional collapse, a detachment from the very fabric that holds our truths to be self-evident and a slap to the core values that our country was founded on.

I am not a martyr; the world will not know of my actions or revel in my sacrifice. Others will continue and thrive, because I have saved them—saved them all—from looking inward. I have hidden their demons and allowed life to go uninterrupted, for I have erased the fear, bagged the chaos, and cleansed the air that was spoiled with death.

This was not just about a monster or a bagful of poop; it's a commentary on our existence and how we treat our planet. And now because someone or something has failed to stand up and take responsibility for their actions, I find myself berating the intelligence and dignity of my fellow man. The fury overwhelms me, and I'm suddenly hit with the staunch realization that perhaps it is I who needs to look inward. What if I am the one too calloused to look into the mirror? What if someone tried to stop it or say something? What if that did happen and the only thing left of them was their sock? Am I to be blamed for a lack of empathy? Dismissal of life? Fear of retribution? How long must I carry this albatross? All these questions begin to pile up, and I'm further now from a resolution than I was five minutes ago! Is this a story of redemption or a misguided allegory? I don't know; I'm tired. My body falls into the familiar comforts of the couch, the couch that will ease my body, clear my head, and allow me to peacefully ponder the existential quagmire that is left behind when a paranormal pile of shit envelops your front lawn.

Big Bad Me

By the time I decided it was "only" five stories high, most of the damage had been done. I'd been standing at the base for several minutes and watched as naïve little humans were dropped in, looped over, and shot out of the tube like fleshy-wet bullets. It felt like a good idea, an opportunity to lasso in my old age mentality and replace it, for just a minute, with youthful exuberance.

Cathy, to her credit, tried to steer my attention elsewhere. She thought the best approach would be to start on a smaller slide and work my way up. She reminded me about the time I spent hobbling around Navy Pier with a crippled equilibrium and chunks of regurgitated elephant ears pasted down the front of my shirt because the carousel looked "harmless enough." Deep down I knew she was right, but the temptation to "hulk out," "man up," or "take the bull by the horns" was overwhelming. The curves, the lines, the laughter— oh man, I knew it was not to be trusted.

You see, I've spent the better part of my life developing the innate ability to steer clear of sketchy situations and the ulterior motives people tend to hide in casual tomfoolery. A few years ago I wouldn't have thought twice about climbing this slide. Common sense begged me to stay away, but an unreasonable amount of curiosity and fraudulent machismo had convinced me otherwise.

"It looks like fun, right? I mean…it's a slide, just a big wet slide. It'll be fun. Right? Right?" I waited for Cathy to agree; she didn't. She only motioned that she and the girls would be waiting for me at the Lazy Lagoon. As they walked away, I grappled with a conscious that I very rarely listen to. Pro. Con. Pro. Con. Con. Con. Con…Oh for the love of God, I've spent thirty-eight years on this Earth, and I know—I *know*—that the best decision is to walk away. But I've also unscientifically assumed that I'm running on a waning reserve of testosterone. Yes, the Lazy Lagoon looked nice, but it didn't look exciting, so…pro! Final answer. I'm gonna handle that slide, and by the time it spits me out, I'll have averted a midlife crisis.

I had little to no emotion while I moseyed up the stairs. I was neither nervous nor excited, just a confident grown-ass man going against my better judgment.

But as I stood in line, I began collecting bits of crucial information that were most definitely overlooked or undisclosed during my decision-making process. First, from the base of the slide, five stories didn't really seem that tall, but as I stood on the platform, I was convinced I could see Germany. Second, you have to step on a huge digital scale before you enter the slide. Your weight and a green light determine whether you are equipped with enough mass to send you through the loop. I mean there's an honest-to-god weight-versus-gravity equation involved! Finally, the door. You didn't just go up, sit on your butt, and gently push yourself down. No, no, no! You stepped into a tube and onto a piece of clear Plexiglas. Then you're told to cross your arms so they won't be separated from your body during the fall! After you're sealed in, it's "Clank! Whoosh! Next?"

The six kids behind me seemed really excited, so I let them cut in front. I let another one jump ahead, because I felt my suit was not properly tied, and when I thought I heard some loose change fall from my pocket, I let a couple more kids go while I looked for it. Then...

"Hey, buddy, you're up." The voice was small and meek. The owner and managing tyrant of that operation was a sixteen-year-old boy. His name was probably Troy, and he wore a red tank top.

I looked over the edge and saw Cathy and the girls waving at me from the Lazy Lagoon. From up there, it looked nice, maybe even a little exciting, but I do not wear defeat well, so I turned to the scale. With one foot on, I was halted by squeaky Troy: "You can just hop right in. You'll go down just fine. Probably faster than most." I wasn't sure if he was being efficient or insulting me. In either case I thanked him, and I proceeded to step onto the clear trap door.

Looking down at my feet, I realized I was floating above the rushing waters, and I watched nervously as they spilled down the throat of this thirsty demon. I immediately regretted my decision to partake in such a ridiculous and callus act of arrogance.

"Cross your arms over your chest and keep them like that until you get to the bottom," yelled the sixteen-year-old button pusher. I nodded, but I don't know why. I no longer wanted to be there. I wanted to step out, but the door began to slowly close around me, causing me to hyperventilate. The rapid release of oxygen started to fog up the clear tube. Suddenly, I remember the scene from *Bill & Ted's Excellent Adventure* where a time-traveling Napoleon has a euphoric waterslide experience at the Waterloo of San Dimas, California. He's smiling, laughing, and slowly twisting through the turns; it's a scene of pure joy. That's what I wanted; that's the kind of slide I should be on, not this! This was some NASA astronaut-training bullshit. I don't wanna be a man; I wanna be a boy. A boy too small to go on this ride. Then I heard a voice.

"Three…" It's a countdown. It was a prerecorded robot-lady voice, and it wasn't comforting. I looked at my feet.

"Two…" It's not a lady; it's the sound of the Devil! It's the voice you hear when you play a Sheryl Crow album backwards! My chin was quivering.

"One." The floor gave way, and for a split second I hovered above the hole like Wile E. Coyote after realizing he has just raced a bit too far over the cliff. Then my body, with little to no resistance, began to fall, leaving my head level and eye-to-eye with Troy. In my mind I held up a sign that read "Yikes!" I tried to let out a scream, but the only sound to come out of my body was a very faint "oh."

The speed at which my body plummeted to Earth had only ever been achieved in a dream. I tried to close my eyes, but the force of resisting air had my eyelids peeling over my forehead. I felt no sense of joy, no exhilaration—just regret. I saw visions of fire, war, steam, babies crying, and raw meat. It was clear that I'd hallucinated myself into a U2 video.

The loop was a nonfactor; I was going way too fast to even remotely comprehend the fact that I'd just defied gravity. My main concern was my swim trunks, which were stuck so far up my ass I could feel mesh on the back of my throat! What started as a small wet wedgie had now progressed so far up my colon that I feared I was about to be ripped lengthwise into two pieces! And then it's done. It's over. I was spit out of the tube and down a long straightaway like so many kids before me.

After I cracked my jaw and unclenched my butt cheeks, I looked to see another Troy boy in a red tank top. I took one look at his angelic face, and I was overcome with emotion. I literally had no idea what to do. He had no sympathy or compassion for what had just happened; he simply told me to move. I stood up, and as I pulled my shorts down off my nipples, I was suddenly overcome by that weird, panicky, "don't let them see you cry in public" feeling. My eyes welled up with tears, and I began that bottom-lip-sucking silent cry you get after having the air knocked out of you. The only legitimate option I had at that point was to run away, run far away from the slide.

By the time the girls stopped me, I'd been frantically meandering through the park for twenty minutes. I was back to my normal shade of pasty white, and my eyes had stopped watering. They were eager to hear about the ride. They asked about the temperature of the water and how many steps there were. They asked how long the line was and if there was a lifeguard. Finally, they asked whether I'd be going back down. I hugged them. I hugged them hard. Cathy had that "I told you so" look on her face. I kissed her and wanted to renew our vows. I asked the girls about the Lazy Lagoon.

"*Boring!*" they both screamed.

"Nice," I replied. "Let's go there."

Eight Years and Two Quarters

The greatest questions are born during the rare instances when the flip of a coin reveals no answer. Neither heads nor tails, the coin stands unabated, upright, and unwilling to give its consent. It's the inexplicable teeter of awe and improbability that allows us to feed our desires to make educated guesses and articulated arguments. It's the spontaneous moments of curiosity that lead us on the path of self-awareness and academic success. As a parent, these are the questions I seek from my daughters. The whos and whats, the wheres and whens, the whys and hows. Those fantastical moments wrought with exhilaration that welcome a dive into an unexplored discussion of middle ground. At least that's how I felt until my eight-year-old daughter asked me to tell her about the first time I got pubic hair.

I had never been more ill prepared for a question in my *life*! Thirty seconds ago we'd been talking about sugar fairies and lip gloss!

"Um, what's that?" I said, hoping to God I had misheard her tired little voice.

"Well, Mommy and I have been reading this book about puberty, and it was talking about getting pubic hair…" I didn't hear anything after that; she may very well have been giving me the directions to a Stargate porthole in a lost Peruvian language for all I know. My heart was racing. Eyes watering, I felt like I was gonna faint.

"Oh, well, ah…go to bed. That's not a nice thing to say. I love you?" I shut the door and left the room.

By the time Cathy got home, I'd sweated through three shirts and chugged down a bottle of room-temperature chardonnay while spinning off twenty-three miles on our stationary bike. I, for lack of a better term, was a disaster.

"You are never gonna believe what your daughter said to me tonight." My tone was firm and slurred. Cathy, who was visibly concerned, put down her bag and rushed over to the bike where I'd been peddlin' and cryin' like a crazy man for the last fifty-three minutes.

"What's going on? Who said what? What'd she say?"

I leaned in close, put my drenched arm around her shoulder, and whispered as light as I could, "Lucy. She said...rather she asked me about"—I clear my throat—"pubic hair."

"Oh? What did you tell her?"

"I told her to go to bed. And I might have told her it wasn't nice. Why would she say such a thing? She's eight! I wigged out and ran. I couldn't bear the thought of a follow-up question."

Cathy rolled her eyes in exasperation and said, "Really? That's what you went with?" She shook her head, explained the book, and told me for the *first* time that she had told Lucy she could come to either of us if she ever had questions, thoughts, curiosities, or blah-blah about puberty. I'm not sure if the nausea I experienced was from my wine-cycling experiment or the fact that my kids were getting to "that age." I mean, I guess I felt slightly better knowing there was a running dialogue rather than a statement of desperation on her behalf, but it just seemed too soon.

Cathy assured me it was fine. "We'll get it all figured out in the morning," she said as she helped me off the bike. "You'll be great!" Her confidence was warming.

"I will be, won't I? I can handle this. I was just caught off guard. I'll just apologize for my crude behavior, let her know she can come to me for anything, and we'll be back to talking about bubblegum and the disgusting nature of 'fruit-on-the-bottom' yogurt in no time."

Boy, was I wrong! In fact, after I apologized to Lucy for my caveman attitude, she became an aggressive landmine of puberty seeking facts and questions. She was a walking onslaught of awkward narration and inappropriately timed inquiries. I found myself answering questions about periods, tampons, and body odor with Mom, Mom, and soap. Then, just as I was settling into a groove of competency, she started stringing together hypothetical situations that fell somewhere between every Dr. Seuss book ever and the *Porky's* trilogy.

"Dad?" she asked.

"Hmmm?" I was leery due to the tone of her voice and the fact that it had been nearly fourteen minutes since our last awkward moment.

"You know how one day I'm gonna start my period?"

"Uhhh-huhhh."

"You know how it will probably happen unexpectedly?"

"Umm, OK…" At this point, I was fairly confident I had no worldly idea how this was gonna play out, but I was hanging in there.

"Well…when it does happen, and if it is unexpected, I hope it happens while we're at Kohl's."

You see? This was not a normal conversation! Nobody in their right mind could think about a follow-up to that specific sequence of words. Yet I was now more curious than anyone *ever* in the history of Earth to find out why my daughter thought Kohl's was a safe haven for early menstruation.

"Oh yeah? Why is that?"

"Well, they have machines that sell tampons in the women's room for a quarter. Just in case, like you never know."

I almost died of joy. It was one of the most logically serious and sweetest things I'd ever heard her say. It was the honest observation of a little girl waiting to enter her place in a big world, and it was perfect.

Parenting, much like life, is a work in progress. It's full of juxtaposition and philosophical nonsense. There is no pamphlet on this planet that can prepare you for the absurdity of raising a child. You just live it innately. Eating because you're hungry, sleeping when you're tired, and loving because it is uncontrollable. I am currently nine years into a lifelong contract with my two girls, and any advice I give is simply for the sake of courtesy.

So, do what feels right, and be prepared to *not* have a plan. It's for that reason alone that I'll always carry two quarters in my pocket every time we go to Kohl's, because "just in case, like you never know."

end

of

stories

Jim Noonan has a degree in Education, a dog named Frank, and is often ridiculed by his family and friends for never wanting to eat outside Lincoln Square—the neighborhood he has lived in for the past seventeen years.

end

of

book

81526849R00062

Made in the USA
San Bernardino, CA
08 July 2018